Fontainebleau

VISITOR'S GUIDE

Amaury Lefébure

Head Curator in charge of Heritage.
Director of the National Museum of the Palace of Fontainebleau.

art lys

© 1998, *art lys* 4 rue Saint-Fiacre, 78000 Versailles

ISBN 2-85495-087-9

Table of Contents

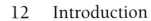

Introduction

Located in the heart of a seventeen thousand hectare forest, the palace of Fontainebleau was once one of the privileged residences of the sovereigns who ruled France. The love of the hunt made it into a regularly-visited residence, and all of its occupants had their hearts set on improving it through new buildings or new decorations. This resulted in the present profusion of courtyards and buildings as well as a rich panorama of architectural and decorative styles.

Although the exact date of its construction is uncertain, it is known that a fortified castle already existed on the site in the 12th century, the only remains of which are the keep in the Oval Courtyard. It was there that the king's bedchamber had been located, lodging such guests as Philippe Auguste (1165-1223), Saint Louis (1214-1270) and Philip the Fair (1268-1314), who died there. Saint Louis was particularly fond of Fontainebleau (his « wilderness » as he called it), where he built a Trinitarian convent/hospital in 1259.

It was in the Renaissance, however, that the palace underwent its most spectacular transformations. François I (1494-1547) fell in love with the site because of the forest, where he could, in his words, devote himself to « the pleasures of the hunt for game of the black and red variety ». His love for Fontainebleau was so great that, whenever he went there, he said that he « was going home ». Starting in 1528, he began the reconstruction and renovation of the palace. While conserving the keep, dating from the Middle Ages, he built, in one area, the Golden Entrance, the Ballroom and Saint Saturnin Chapel (on the Oval Courtyard). He also constructed the buildings encircling the current White Horse Courtyard, on land bought from the Trinitarians; as well as the so-called François I Gallery to link the two groupings of buildings. His son, Henri II (1519-1559), and later, Henri II's wife, Catherine de' Medici (1519-1589), continued the work undertaken by François I and added other buildings in the Fountain Courtyard. To decorate these new constructions, François I called upon the services of Italian artists, namely, a Florentine, Rosso (1494-1540) and a Bolognese, Primaticcio (1504-1570), both founders of what is called the First Fontainebleau School, of which the principal remaining examples are the François I Gallery, the Duchesse d'Etampes's bedchamber and the Ballroom.

Furthermore, François I brought together extremely diverse collections of art work at Fontainebleau : paintings by Leonardo da Vinci (including The Mona Lisa), Andrea del Sarto, Raphael, as well as sculptures, tapestries, precious stones and curios (these collections are now housed at the Louvre museum and the French national library). He thus made Fontainebleau into an artistic center, attracting people from all across Europe. Under François I as well as under his successors, the palace served as the setting for magnificent balls, described by the poet Ronsard (1524-1585) : « When shall we see throughout Fontainebleau/the masquerades going from room to room ».

Henri IV (1553-1610) also played an important role in Fontainebleau's history. He was responsible for the brick and stonework wing facing Diana's Garden, which includes the Deer Gallery and the Queen's (or Diana's) Gallery, the Dauphin's (or Baptistery) Entrance and the buildings on the Kitchen Courtyard. The Second Fontainebleau School dates from this period, in which Flemish artists (Ambroise Dubois, 1543-1614) and French artists (Toussaint Dubreuil, 1561-

1602, Martin Fréminet, 1567-1619) decorated, most notably, the king's bedchamber (the current Louis XIII Salon), the Deer Gallery, the Queen's gallery and the vault of the Trinity Chapel. Louis XIII (1601-1643) had the decoration of the Trinity Chapel completed and reconstructed the famous horseshoe-shaped staircase (actually, a double horseshoe). Under the regency of his wife, Anne of Austria (1601-1666), the State Apartments were embellished with sumptuous sculpted, painted and gilded ceilings.

Louis XIV (1638-1715) scheduled the court's residence at Fontainebleau for every autumn, during hunting season. This schedule of court stays from September to November was maintained until the end of the Ancien Régime. Besides refurbishing the dwellings for an ever-increasing court, Louis XIV ordered the restoration of the apartment in the Golden Entrance (1686) for Madame de Maintenon. Louis XV (1710-1774) and later Louis XVI (1754-1793) initiated substantial new work projects. Under Louis XV, the need to provide lodgings for the court led to the remodelling of the south wing of the White Horse Courtyard, and the construction of the Great Pavilion was the start of the renovation of the palace. With regard to the palace interior, Louis XV modified the layout and the decor of his apartments, installing the King's Staircase, a new Council Chamber, new wainscoting in the king's and queen's bedchambers, and by cutting large doors in the antechambers. Louis XVI, wishing to enlarge the royal apartments, doubled the size of the François I Gallery on Diana's Garden. His wife, Marie Antoinette (1755-1793) had her suite of three apartments (gameroom, bedroom and boudoir) redecorated in keeping with the tastes of the times.

After the Revolution, Napoleon (1769-1821) found the palace completely emptied of its furnishings. From 1803 to 1808, he set up the Special Military School (later transferred to Saint Cyr) in the Louis XV wing ; and beginning in 1804, he refurnished the entire palace, first to receive the Pope, later to make Fontainebleau into one of his favorite residences, refurbishing the Small Apartments for his private use and for that of his wife, Empress Josephine (1763-1814) then after their divorce in 1809, for Empress Marie-Louise (1791-1847). He intended that the State Apartments be specifically used for receptions and ceremonies. Thus, he transformed the king's bedchamber first into a salon and then into the Throne Room (in 1808) and had the imperial apartment sumptuously refurnished. With regard to the palace exterior, he replaced the buildings which enclosed the westerly end of the White Horse Courtyard with a gate that is still there today, and began the renovation of Diana's Gallery--which had fallen into ruins--and which was completed under Louis XVIII.

Louis Philippe (1773-1850) also undertook an ambitious restoration, refurnishing and redecorating program (paintings in the Guardroom and the Gallery of Plates). Napoleon III (1808-1873) completed the refurnishing and he also had a new performance room constructed (1854-1856) in the Louis XV Wing, and Empress Eugénie (1826-1920) installed new salons and a Chinese Museum on the ground level of the Great Pavilion (1863).

While today's visitor may be surprised to find so many juxtaposed periods at Fontainebleau, he can not fail to appreciate the charm of this overall effect. Napoleon, from his last exile at St. Helena, recalled Fontainebleau fondly : « Here was a true home of kings, the house of the centuries » he said. « Perhaps it was not, strictly speaking, an architect's palace, but it was most assuredly a well-thought out and perfectly suitable place of residence. Without a doubt, it was the most comfortable, best-situated one in Europe...».

Historic events

Saint Louis
(1214-1270)

Philippe IV the Fair
(1268-1314)

François I
(1494-1547)

Henri II
(1519-1559)

Henri IV
(1553-1610)

1137- The palace is mentioned for the first time in a charter issued under king Louis VII.

1169- Consecration of the palace's chapel, under the dual patronage of the Virgin and Saint Saturnin, by Saint Thomas Becket, Archbishop of Canterbury, while in exile in France.

1259- Saint Louis founds a Trinitarian convent near the palace.

1268- Birth of Philip IV the Fair at Fontainebleau.

1314- Death of Philip IV the Fair at Fontainebleau

1539- Charles the Fifth stays from December 24 to 30.

1544- Birth of François (the future François II), son of dauphin Henri and Catherine de' Medici.

1551- Birth of Edouard-Alexandre (the future Henri III), fourth son of Henri II and Catherine de Medici.

1560- Notables summoned to meeting in order to pacify religious unrest; they decide to call a meeting of the States General.

1564- Carnival festivities, celebrated by Ronsard.

1601- Birth of the dauphin (the future Louis XIII).

1606- Christening of the dauphin and his sisters in the Oval Courtyard.

Louis XIII
(1601-1643)

1629- Peace treaty between France and England.

Construction of the palace of Fontainebleau

The Keep (12th c., transformed in the 16th c).

The Golden Entrance
(1528).

Fine Fireplace wing constructed by Primaticcio, circa 1565-1570.

Dauphin's Entrance constructed circa 1601-1606.

1700 ————————————————→ **1800** ————→ **1900**

Louis XIV
(1638-1715)

1657- Visit by Queen Christina of Sweden, who has her equerry, Monaldsechi, assassinated.

1661- Birth of the Grand Dauphin, the son of Louis XIV and Maria Theresa of Austria.

1685- Revocation of the Edict of Nantes.

1686-Death of Louis of Bourbon, Prince of Condé, called the Grand Condé.

1700- Louis XIV decides to accept the crown of Spain for his grandson, the Duke of Anjou.

Louis XV
(1710-1774)

1717- Visit by Czar Peter the Great.

1725- Marriage of Louis XV and Maria Leczinska.

1752- Première of J.-J. Rousseau's *Devin du village.*

1765- Death of the son of Louis XV.

Louis XVI
(1754-1793)

1786- Commercial treaty between France and England.

Napoléon I
(1769-1821)

1803- Bonaparte, First Consul, organizes the Special Military School, which will move to Saint Cyr in 1808.

1804- Napoléon receives Pope Pius VII, who has come for the coronation.

1812- Second stay of Pope Pius VII, who is placed under house arrest (for 19 months) by Napoleon.

1813- Fontainebleau Concordat on January 25th.

1814- On April 6, unconditional abdication of Napoleon I. April 20th, Napoleon's departure for the Isle of Elba. Farewell speech to his guards.

Louis-Philippe
(1773-1850)

1837- Marriage of Ferdinand-Philippe, Duke of Orléans, eldest son of Louis-Philippe and Helène de Mecklembourg-Schwerin.

Napoléon III
(1808-1873)

1861- Reception for the ambassadors of the King of Siam.

1921- Creation of the American Conservatory.

1923- Creation of the American School of Fine Arts.

1946- Franco-Vietnamese conference

1948- Creation of the International Union for the Protection of Nature.

1949/1966- Installation of the NATO Supreme Headquarters, in part of the palace.

1984- Metting of the heads of state and governments of the European Economic Community.

The pavilion in Carp Pond is constructed by Le Vau in 1662.

The Great Pavilion constructed by Gabriel in 1750-1754.

Railing fence of the White Horse Courtyard erected in 1809-1810.

Chinese Museum installed in 1863.

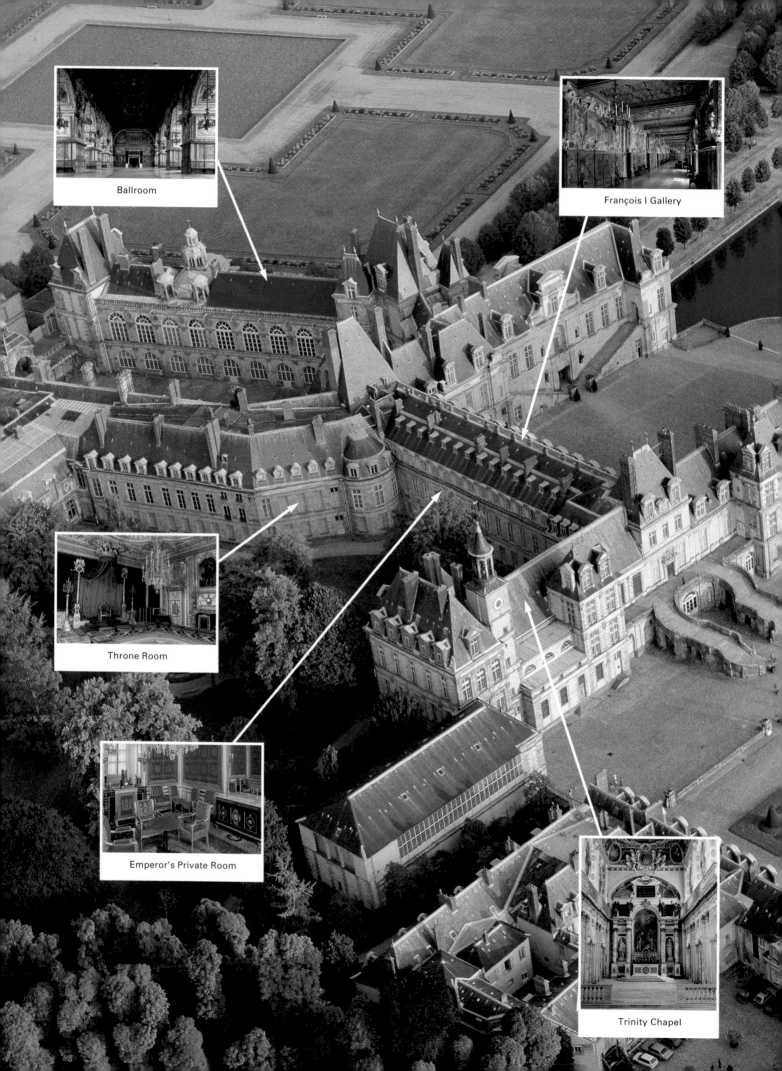

Ballroom

François I Gallery

Throne Room

Emperor's Private Room

Trinity Chapel

Empress Eugénie's Salons
and the Chinese Museum

Napoleon I Museum

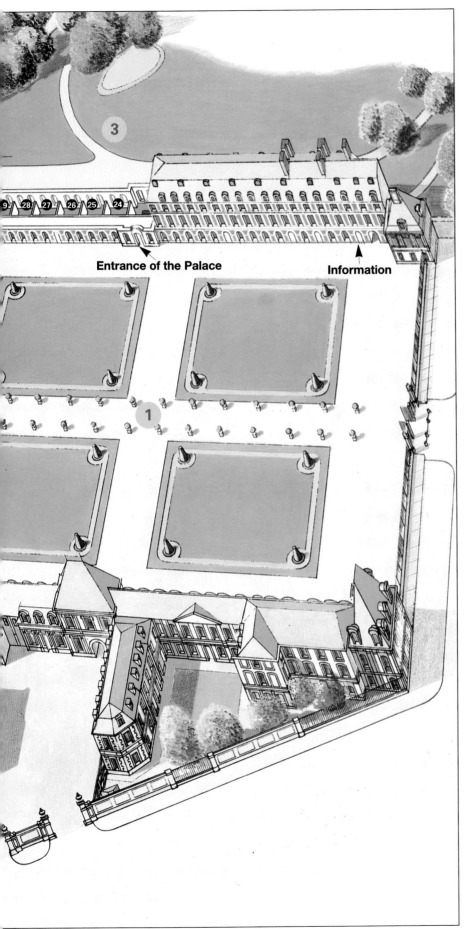

Layout of the Ground Level

State Apartments

1 Trinity Chapel

Small Apartments

2 Emperor's Antechamber
3 Emperor's First Salon
4 Emperor's Second Salon
5 Méneval's Room
6 Emperor's Wardrobe Room
7 Room of the Emperor's *gardien du portefeuille*
8 Emperor's Bedroom
9 Connecting Room
10 Emperor's 3rd Office
11 Emperor's 2nd Office
12 Emperor's 1st Office
13 Swan's Neck Antechamber
14 Map Room
15 Empress's Study
16 Empress's Bedroom
17 Empress's Bathroom
18 Service Passage
19 Empress's Second Salon
20 Empress's Firs Salon or Billiard Room
21 Passage
22 Empress's Antechamber
23 Deer Gallery

Napoleon I Museum

24 Room IX : Emperor's Mother
25 Room X : Joseph
26 Room XI : Louis
27 Room XI : Jérôme
28 Room XIII : Elisa
29 Room XIV : Pauline
30 Room XV : Caroline

Empress Eugénie's Salons and the Chinese Museum

Courtyards and Gardens

① White Horse Courtyard

② Fountain Courtyard

③ English Garden

④ Grand Parterre

⑤ Oval Courtyard

⑥ Diana's Garden

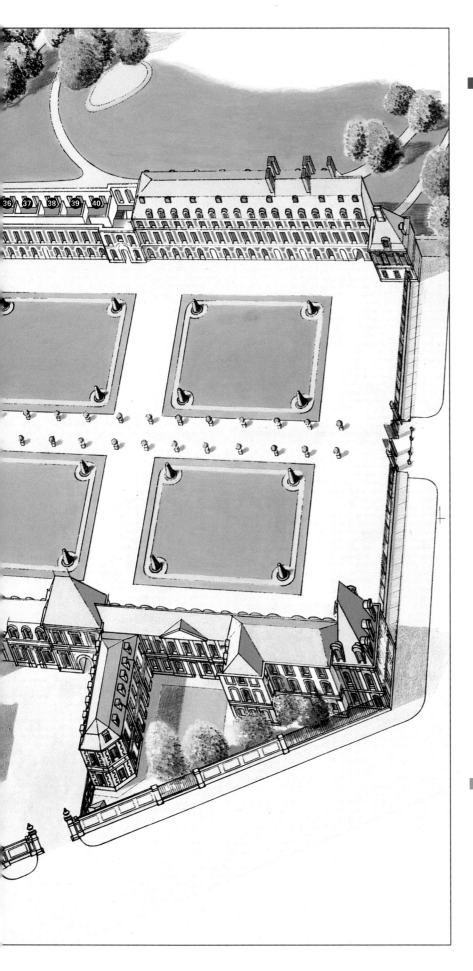

Layout of first floor

State Apartments and Renaissance Rooms

1 Stucco Staircase
2 Antechamber of the Gallery of Splendor
3 Gallery of Splendor
4 Gallery of Plates
5 Horseshoe Vestibule
6 François I Gallery
7 Guardroom
8 Louis XV Salon
9 Madame de Maintenon's Apartment
10 Ballroom
11 Saint-Saturnin Chapel
12 Madame d'Étampes's Bedchamber or King's Staircase
13 Rotunda
14 First Saint Louis Room
15 Second Saint Louis Room
16 Louis XIII Salon
17 François I Salon
18 Tapestry Salon
19 Empress's Antechamber
20 Diana's Gallery
21 White Salon
22 Queen's Gameroom or Empress's Grand Salon
23 Empress's Bedchamber
24 Queen's Boudoir
25 Throne Room
26 Council Chamber

Napoleon I's Imperial Apartment

27 Emperor's Bedchamber
28 Emperor's Small Bedroom
29 Emperor's Private Room or Abdication Room
30 Passage to Emperor's bathrooms
31 Room of the Emperor's Aides-de-Camp
32 Emperor's Antechamber

Napoleon I Museum

33 Room I : Napoleon : Emperor and King
34 Room II : Splendors of the Imperial Table
35 Room III : Gifts Presented to the Emperor
36 Room IV : The Emperor and his Military Campaigns
37 Room V : The Emperor's Daily Life
38 Room VI : Marie-Louise
39 Room VII : The King of Rome
40 Room VIII : The King of Rome

The Courtyards

Fontainebleau palace spreads across four main court-yards, each in succession from west to east and covering a surface area of more than three hectares. The diversity of the buildings is testimony of the successive construction programs undertaken from the 16th until the 19th century.

White Horse Courtyard

This is now the palace's main entrance courtyard. It once was the site of a convent, founded by Saint Louis, which François I annexed to the palace of the kings of France, starting in 1528. The main façade, in back, includes the Trinity Chapel which has replaced the former gothic abbey.

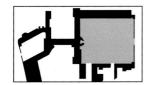

The horseshoe staircase wing took its final shape in the years between 1544-1565, but the layout of the buildings underwent constant alteration until the 19th century.

The Gate of Honor (1809-1810) is richly ornamented with Napoleonic emblems. The two gilt iron eagles, which were removed in 1814 and 1870, were permanently reinstalled in 1911.

The name of the White Horse Courtyard derives from a plaster horse, inspired by an antique equestrian statue of Marcus Aurelius in Rome. Erected in the period of Catherine de' Medici, it disappeared after 1626. This courtyard is also called the Farewell Courtyard in memory of Napoleon's farewell ceremony before his departure for the Isle of Elba, which was held at the foot of the horseshoe staircase on April 20, 1814.

A horseshoe staircase was first constructed during the reign of Henri II by Philibert Delorme. The present-day staircase was built between 1632 and 1634 by Jean Androuet Du Cerceau to replace the 16th century staircase in disrepair.

The Louis XV wing (1739-1740 and 1773-1774), built in brick and stone, replaced a 16th century (where the famous Gallery of Ulysses was located) wing similar to the lower wing (called the Ministers' Wing) which borders the north side of the courtyard.

Fountain Courtyard

Well-situated in front of Carp Pond, the Fountain Courtyard is bordered by three wings. The courtyard owes its architectural unity to the use of one material, Saint-Leu stone, and the general arrangement of the façades. Voussoirs, corner stones, windows and dormer windows echo the façade of the Queen Mothers' Wing, while the pattern of double pilasters and niches of the ground-level corner pavilions of the Fine Fireplace Wing was repeated in the terrace of the François I Gallery.

Constructed starting in 1528, the wing of the François I Gallery linked the royal apartments located around the Oval Courtyard, to the east, with the buildings of the White Horse Courtyard. François I had a bathroom suite installed on the ground level and above the famous gallery which still exists today.

The Fine Fireplace Wing (circa
1565-1570), by Primaticcio,
owes its originality to the two
straight-ramp staircases,
no doubt inspired by the
works of Bramante at the
Vatican and Michelangelo
at the Capitol.

A fountain, constructed
in 1541 by Primaticcio,
surmounted by a statue of
Hercules by Michelangelo,
no longer remains.
The present fountain
dates from 1812.
The statue of Ulysses
by Petitot (1819) was
installed in 1824.

The Queen Mothers' Wing (1558-1566), to the west, was constructed
under the direction of Philibert Delorme and later Primaticcio. The
Great Pavilion at the far corner of the wing replaced in 1750 a 16th
century pavilion. The Great Pavilion is the work of Louis XV's architect,
Ange-Jacques Gabriel ; and its decor was inspired by the art work at
Versailles.

The Oval Courtyard

This is the oldest part of the palace, still dominated by the square-shaped Keep from the 12th century (later rebuilt). The buildings surrounding it were built on the foundations of the original medieval castle.

The Dauphin's Entrance is also called the Baptistery Entrance in commemoration of the baptism of Louis XIII, which took place in the Oval Courtyard on September 14, 1606.

The buildings dating from the time of François I extend from both sides of the Keep, to the north as far as the so-called Serlio portico, and to the south as far as the Saint Saturnin Chapel, recognizable by campaniles. The two grand pavilions and the new triumphal entrance, called the Dauphin's Entrance, were built on the east side under Henri IV.

The Kitchen or Henri IV Courtyard

The Kitchen Courtyard (1606-1609) is surrounded on three sides by alternating high and low buildings with sandstone, brick and quarry stone fronting, whose most remarkable elements are the central pavilion of the southern wing, with its curved façade, and the grand entrance to the north.

Two heads of Mercury, the god of travelers and who watched over roads and crossroads (sculpted by Gilles Guérin in 1639), stand above the passageway between the Kitchen Courtyard and the Oval Courtyard.

The buildings of the Kitchen Courtyard housed the officers' pantries and living quarters. The courtyard itself served as the entrance area where court members who were not of noble blood, marshals or ambassadors, were required to leave their coaches or dismount, before entering the Oval Courtyard.

State Apartments

After entering the palace through the central pavilion of the Louis XV wing, the visitor walks along the hall of the ground floor and climbs a richly decorated stucco staircase made to look like marble. Constructed in 1866-1868, this staircase is lighted by a bronze gilded lantern dating from the Louis XV period, attributed to J. Caffieri.

Antechamber of the Gallery of Celebrations

The decor of this room dates from the Second Empire, as do the stained-glass window and the two vases, one of which is decorated with a depiction of warriors and the other by women surrounded by cupids. These vases, as well as the one on the landing, are in Sèvres porcelain.

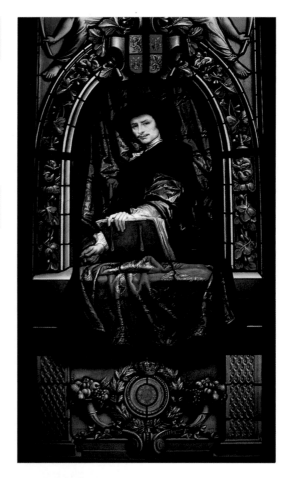

Napoleon III bought this stained glass window by Laurent-Charles Maréchal, titled *L'Artiste*, at the Universal Exposition of 1867. After the Emperor's monogram and the date were added, it was installed at this location in 1869.

This painting was commissioned by Louis XV from the painter Jean-Baptiste Oudry. The king wished to have portraits made of his favorite dogs. Here, Oudry, who was a specialist in the genre, has painted *Mignonne and Sylvie*, two greyhounds from Louis XV's kennel. Executed in 1728, this painting was originally placed above the door.

The various paintings hung facing the windows recreate the room's appearance at the end of the Second Empire. Among them can be noted two paintings by Jean Lemaire (1598-1659), an artist influenced by Poussin, *Women at dance in a Palace* and *Colonnade of a Palace in Ruins*.

Gallery of Celebrations

This gallery was created under the reign of Napoleon III at the site of a staircase and vestibule, in order to link the Gallery of Plates to the Louis XV wing. On the basis of an idea suggested by Napoleon III, the walls of this room were to be decorated with paintings representing historic scenes which took place at Fontainebleau ; hence the name Gallery of Celebrations. However, ultimately, only the ceiling was painted, with a depiction of imperial arms, by A. Denuelle in 1866-1867.

J-L Demarne and A-M Dunouy, *Meeting between Napoleon and Pope Pius VII in the forest of Fontainebleau*, detail (1808). This event took place on November 25, 1804, on the occasion of the Pope's arrival for the religious ceremony for the Emperor's coronation.

A-L-R. Millin du Perreux, *Henri IV's defense of Sully at Fontainebleau* (1819). The minister, falsely accused of treason, is supported by the King, in the presence of the court which is assembled under the trees along the shore of Carp Pond.

Several of the paintings now on display are faithful to Napoleon III's idea : *Louis XIII's Christening at Fontainebleau* (Cl. Boulanger, 1834), *Allegory to the Death of the Dauphin* (L. Lagrenée, 1767), depicting the death of the son of Louis XV and father of Louis XVI, who died at Fontainebleau in 1765.

Gallery of Plates

Under the reign of Louis Philippe, this gallery was built in 1840, replacing a terrace, in order to facilitate movement through this part of the palace. Frescoes from the vault of Diana's Gallery (see p. 40) were transferred onto canvas and installed on the ceiling and walls. These paintings were done by A. Dubois and his studio (circa 1600-1605) and represent mythological divinities and children participating in the hunt.

Plate of Sèvres porcelain from the Fontainebleau history plate service, depicting François I welcoming Benvenuto Cellini to Fontainebleau in 1540.

Chest commemorating the marriage of the Duke of Orléans to Princess Hélène de Mecklembourg-Schwerin, in Sèvres porcelain (1841).

On display in the gallery is a porcelain chest which was originally in the apartment of the Duchess of Orléans.

Louis Philippe had one-hundred and twenty-eight Sèvres porcelain plates, known as the Fontainebleau history plates (1839-1844), displayed in the Renaissance style wainscoting. These plates, which were never used, depicted views of the palace and the forest or events which occurred there, as well as views of other royal residences or foreign places visited by Louis Philippe.

Plate in Sèvres porcelain from the Fontainebleau history plates depicting Diana's Garden, in 1842, with the fountain as Napoleon had reconstructed it.

King Louis Philippe receiving Princess Hélène de Mecklembourg-Schwerin at the top of the horseshoe staircase.
A commemorative case plate of Sèvres porcelain, depicting the marriage of the Duke of Orléans, painted by Develly. The wedding of the Duke of Orléans, the king's eldest son and heir to the throne, took place on May 30, 1837, and was celebrated with lavish ceremonies. Following the wishes of Louis Philippe, the palace had undergone extensive restorations.

Renaissance Rooms

At the time of the Renaissance, Fontainebleau palace was one of the major artistic centers of 16th century Europe. Several groups of works dating from the reigns of François I and Henri II have survived.

François I Gallery

This gallery is located in a wing built in 1528, to provide a passage between the royal apartments and the chapel of the Trinitarian convent founded by Saint Louis near the palace. Initially reserved for use by the king, it later became a public passageway.

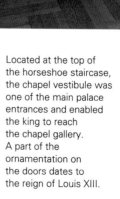

Located at the top of the horseshoe staircase, the chapel vestibule was one of the main palace entrances and enabled the king to reach the chapel gallery. A part of the ornamentation on the doors dates to the reign of Louis XIII.

60 meters long and
6 meters wide, the gallery
was originally illuminated
on both sides. The northern
windows were sealed in
1785, at the time of the
construction of an adjacent
wing.

The salamander, François I's emblem and mascot, and symbol of man's perseverance in the face of adversity, appears on the sculpted and gilded walnut wainscoting.

Each bay of the gallery is decorated, above the wainscoting, by frescoes whose rich stucco framing contains an infinite variety of human figures and vegetable motifs.

For the decor of the gallery, François I commissioned an Italian artist, Rosso, a great admirer of Michelangelo. Working with a team of French, Italian and Flemish painters and sculptors, Rosso developed a decorating style that united fresco painting and stucco sculpture with wainscoting.

The stucco ornamentation bears some relation to the frescoes it frames. For example, the male and female satyrs (shown at left) symbolize the vices (lust) to which those who are ignorant yield (in the fresco shown below). Their impressive bearing and size are typical of the mannerist style.

One of the framing motifs used systematically throughout the decor of the gallery played an important role in the history of decorative arts: *cuir découpé* (fretted leatherwork).

The iconographic impact of the images, heightened by references to antiquity, is also intended to convey a moral and religious meaning. The gallery illustrates the proper role of the king, to avoid dangers and seek peace and unity. François I seems to be depicted above as a humane and virtuous ruler entering the Temple of Jupiter triumphantly, while those who prefer to remain in ignorance are lost.

Ajax's shipwreck is an episode from the Trojan War, which may be interpreted as an allegory of the perils that the king may surmount through virtue.

Here, the elephant decorated with the fleur-de-lys represents François I. This animal is the image of power that extends over the entire earth and dominates the other elements. Air is symbolized by Jupiter's lightning, water by Neptune's trident, and fire by Cerberus (the three-headed dog of the pagan hell), visible at the feet of the three figures surrounding the elephant.

Madame de Maintenon's Apartment

Madame de Maintenon, who secretly married Louis XIV in 1683 ; shortly after the death of the queen, lived in this apartment from 1686 until 1714. The king visited the apartment frequently and often worked here with his ministers until late into the night.

Grand Salon

This room was the bedchamber of Madame de Maintenon. A part of the wainscoting dates from the renovations made for her. The royal sun is visible. However, the red damask furniture, mentioned on the inventory lists from that period, have disappeared.

The Guardroom provides passage from the François I Gallery to the Ballroom and Madame de Maintenon's Apartment (occasionally open).

The bed and chairs, of royal provenance, date from the reign of Louis XVI, whereas the commode adorned with Boulle marquetry dates from the end of the reign of Louis XIV, and was purchased for the room in 1837.

The Louis XIV chairs,
covered in ancient tapestry,
and the Boulle marquetry
desk from the end of
the 17th century were
installed during
the Second Empire.

Loggia

The loggia is located on the first floor of the Golden Entrance constructed during the reign of François I. Glass panes were installed in the bay in 1661, in order to make the apartment more comfortable. From the loggia, on hunting nights, Madame de Maintenon could observe the stag kills which were often performed just below its windows.

Armchair by Sené and
Vallois, recovered in Empire
satin (rewoven in 1982),
from Marie Antoinette's
private study at
Saint Cloud (1787).

Bedchamber

The room is today as it was during the reign of Louis Philippe. At the time it was occupied by the king's sister, Madame Adélaide; later, during the Second Empire, it was occupied by Napoleon III's cousin, Princess Mathilde. The gilded wood bed was delivered to Fontainebleau in 1787, for Madame Elisabeth, Louis XVI's sister.

Renaissance Rooms

After the death of François I, his son Henri II continued the palace renovations, by finishing the buildings in progress and by initiating new construction. The work was entrusted to the architect Philibert Delorme and the artist Primaticcio.

Ballroom

Begun under François I, this room was originally to be covered by a barrel vault. Delorme substituted a coffered ceiling, inspired by Italian models. Numerous festivities were held in this room until the reign of Louis XIII, and then once again in the 19th century.

The monumental fireplace is the work of Delorme and included two bronze satyrs, based on antique models, which were sculpted in François I's time by Primaticcio (they were melted during the Revolution and recast in 1966). At the balls, the king would stand on a platform, with his back to the fireplace.

Henri II's monogram appears throughout the decor, combined with the crescent of the moon (emblem of the king) and a letter which is visible, C, (initial of Queen Catherine de' Medici), or D (Diane de Poitiers, the King's mistress).

The Ballroom is 30 meters long and 10 meters wide. Through ten large bay windows, the ballroom opens to the north onto the Oval Courtyard, the oldest of the palace's courtyards, and to the south to the Grand Parterre.

The Three Graces Dancing before the Gods.
The subject of this work suggests the intended purpose of the room, in which a musician's gallery was to be built above the entrance door.

The frescoes on the walls, based on drawings by Primaticcio, were executed in the 1550's, by a team headed by Nicolo dell'Abbate. Greatly damaged over the centuries, the frescoes were restored on several occasions. The scenes depict mythological subjects or allegories of the hunt.

Saint Saturnin Chapel

Originally founded by Saint Thomas Becket during his exile in France in 1169, the Saint Saturnin Chapel was entirely reconstructed under the reign of François I, according to an original plan, providing for an apse at each end.

The chapel is noteworthy for its exceptional vaulting. One of the keystones bears the date of 1546. The painted ornamentation, which bears the monogram of King Henri IV and of Queen Marie de' Medeci, dates from 1608. The lantern was reconstructed in 1882.

The gallery, intended to serve as an organ loft, was built during Henri II's reign, by Delorme, who had it supported by two Ionic columns in marble, carved in 1554.

Nature, a marble statue by Tribolo, commissioned in 1529 for François I, to serve as a support for a bowl and displayed by the king at Fontainebleau.

Madame d'Etampes's Bedchamber or the King's Staircase

This room was the bedchamber of Madame d'Estampes, who was François I's favorite. The frescoes and stucco work on the walls, based on the theme of the story of Alexandre and Roxane, were completed between 1541 and 1544 by Primaticcio. In 1749 the room was transformed into a staircase by Louis XV's architect, Gabriel.

The Sovereigns' State Apartments

The Sovereigns' State Apartments consist of the rooms of the king's and queen's apartments, intended for the activity of the court. Access was subject to the rules of court etiquette, entry to certain rooms was granted to members of the court based on their rank.

Guardroom

The king's bodyguards in charge of monitoring entry resided here. The military nature of their functions is suggested by the ornamentation on the frieze (military trophies) at the top of the walls. The furniture is that which was installed there during the Second Empire, when the room could be used as a dining room.

The Renaissance style wall decoration, painted in 1834-1836, is devoted to several sovereigns from the 16th and 17th centuries (François I, Henri II, Henri IV, Louis XIII), depicted with their arms, their monograms and those of their spouses, their emblems and their mottoes, and the names and dates of their victories.

The ceiling (circa 1570, redesigned under Louis XIII), inspired the rest of the decor, which was redone during the reign of Louis Philippe. The fireplace is surmounted by a bust of Henri IV, attributed to Mathieu Jacquet (circa 1600).

First Saint Louis Room
Second Saint Louis Room

Named to commemorate the visits of the king, Saint Louis, these two rooms occupy part of the « kings dwelling » which, from the Middle Ages until the 16th century, housed the « room » of the king (1st room) and the king's bedchamber (2nd room). During the 17th and 18th centuries, they served when the king ate his meals in public using the Grand Table Service.

Clock attributed to Boulle and his sons, circa 1725, decorated by a group of figures from Apollo's Chariot that was inspired by the statue in the Apollo basin at Versailles and installed in this room in 1837.

Henri IV on horseback, bas relief in marble by M. Jacquet (circa 1600), from Fontainebleau's famous Fine Fireplace (destroyed during Louis XV's reign, reinstalled here in 1836).

The current layout of these two rooms (the second room is located in the keep) dates from 1757, when Louis XV had the walls cut to create the arcade joining the rooms. The wainscoting and ceiling coffers date from this period but were repainted and embellished in 1836 by gilded *carton-papier* ornamentation and paintings, notably by A. Dubois (beginning of the 17th century) and Fr.-A Vincent (scenes from the life of Henri IV, 1783-87).

Louis XIII Salon

It was here that the future Louis XIII was born on September 27, 1601. Shortly after his birth, his father Henri IV had the room redecorated. The paintings on the walls and the coffered ceiling by Ambrose Dubois represent the Romance between Theagenes and Chariclea, as recounted in a Greek novel that was famous of the 17th century. The four large doors were added under Louis XV, when the room became antechamber. Up until that time, this room was the king's study where he worked and gave audiences.

Under Louis XIV, some of the court gathered in this room after the king's supper. The Duke of Saint-Simon noted in his memoirs that the ladies were forced to assume uncomfortable positions in order to comply with the rules of etiquette : « the ladies of honor, seated duchesses, joining the princesses [...] the others standing or seated on the parquet floor, where not even a cushion was provided to the Marshal of Rochefort ».

The wainscoting, perhaps executed by Flemish artists, is decorated with representations of more than one hundred different varieties of flowers, both in their natural state and in arranged bouquets, and fruits.

The furniture, in part from the 17th century and in part from the 19th century, was installed during the Second Empire when the room served as a salon. The lightweight chairs, in natural or gilded wood (1858) could be easily moved.

The Capture of the Fox. Hunt in Scotland. Bronze group by the animal sculptor, P.-J. Mène (1861).

François I Salon

This room was the queen's bedroom in the 16th century, prepared for the second wife of François I, Eleanor of Austria, the sister of Charles the Fifth. The room became an antechamber sometime around 1565, and in the 17th and 18th centuries served as the room of the Grand Table Service for the queen or as a concert hall. It was later used as a dining room.

Ebony cabinet (Paris, circa 1645) known as the Odyssey Cabinet, because of the interior decorations which are based on engravings of the scenes found in the former Ulysses's Gallery at Fontainebleau.

Fireplace decorated with stucco and frescoes executed by Primaticcio between 1534 and 1537. The central medallion represents the marriage of Venus and Adonis and is based on a drawing by Giulio Romano.

Only the fireplace and the ceiling (restored in the 19th century) remain of the 16th century decor. The present furnishings were installed during the Second Empire : tapestries of the *Hunts of Maximilian*, woven in Gobelins during the reign of Louis XIV, inspired by the famous tapestries in the Louvre ; chairs and table in gilded wood, in the Louis XIV style, installed in 1852 and 1860 ; part of the Savonnerie rug from the Tuileries Throne Room (1818).

Tapestry Salon

This room served for a long time as the queen's guard-room. Transformed into a salon under the reign of Louis-Philippe, it was given a new Renaissance style ceiling made of pine, and decorated with tapestries, accounting for its name. The tapestries presently in place , as well as the rest of the furnishings, were installed during the Second Empire. The tapestries recount the myth of Psyche and were woven in Paris in the middle of the 17th century. The Savonnerie rug (1817) was made for the Tuileries. The Boulle style furniture dates from 1839-1840.

Empress's Antechamber

Since 1768, after the installation of a staircase constructed by Louis XV (which is located behind the door near the windows) this room has provided the means of access to the sovereigns' private rooms. Like all the rooms in this suite on the Oval Courtyard, it has maintained its Second Empire appearance. The Gobelins tapestries (1673), based on cartoons by Le Brun, represent three of *The Seasons, Summer, Autumn* and *Winter*; in *Summer*, near the bottom, the Carp Pond at Fontainebleau is recognizable.

Diana's Gallery

The decoration of this room which Henri IV had built for his queen, is devoted to the myth of Diana and the king's victories. In ruins in the beginning of the 19th century, the room was reconstructed by Napoleon I and its new decor finished during the Restoration. M.-J. Blondel and A. Abel de Pujol portrayed once again in this room the myth of Diana.

The Diana's Gallery in 1839, watercolor by Th. Allom. At that time, the walls of a part of the gallery were decorated with scenes from the history of the French monarchy.

It took ten years to complete this vase made of Sèvres porcelain (1822-1832), which depicts the studio of the Greek sculptor Phidias with the statue of Jupiter.

Diana's Gallery, 80 meters long and 7 meters wide, was converted into a library by Napoleon III in 1858. It contains nearly 16,000 volumes from the library of Napoleon I at Fontainebleau (which had been located in the Saint-Saturnin Chapel, but no longer remains). The globe of the world, placed here in 1861, was made for Napoleon I in 1810, and used by him at the Tuileries Palace.

White Salon

This room formerly contained a cabinet decorated by Dubois for Marie de' Medici, but it was removed during the reign of Louis XV. The room in its current state was arranged by Louis Philippe in 1835, to serve as a small salon for Queen Marie-Amélie and is fitted with Louis XV wainscoting and a Louis XVI fireplace.

Pedestral table made of Sevres pocelain (1803-1806). In the center of the table top Apollo is depicted driving the Sun Chariot. Around are the seasons.

The furniture surrounding the pedestal table made at the end of the 18th century, is from the period of the Consulate (armchairs and other chairs by the Jacob brothers; circa 1800) or the Empire (flower stand by Thomire and clock in Sèvres porcelain, 1810 ; screen by Marcion, 1813).

Queen's Gameroom
or Empress's Grand Salon

In this room, originally called the Queen's Grand Study, the queen gave official audiences and concerts. Marie Antoinette had the decor entirely redone in a neoclassical style by the architect Pierre Rousseau in 1786. The ceiling painted by J.S. Barthélemy represents Minerva crowning the muses. During this period, the room was used for the queen's games, and included 12 tables for lotto, three-of-a-kind, piquet and quadrille, and a backgammon board. During the Empire, it became the Empress's Grand Salon, and new furnishings were designed to conform to the strict rules of etiquette.

The room is presented alternately with two different furnishings, either as it was under Louis XVI or as it was during the First Empire. Among the Louis XVI furnishings are two viewers (*voyeuses*) in painted wood, which were used when kneeling to survey the game. Among the Empire furniture, the armchairs were reserved for the Emperor and the Empress, the chairs for the princesses, and the stools and the folding seats for the ladies.

Empress's Bedchamber

This room was the bedchamber for all the queens and empresses from perhaps as early as the end of the 16th century and up until as late as 1870. It appears today as it was decorated for Empress Josephine and as it was known by the last sovereign to have lived there, Empress Eugénie.

On the occasion of the reconstruction of the room in its Empire decor (in 1986), the initial « J » for Josephine was restored here to a tieback of the bedcurtains.

Different parts of the decor were designed for different sovereigns : for Anne of Austria, the central part of the ceiling, 1644, for Marie Leczinska, the alcove ceiling, fireplace, overmantel, lower wainscoting, 1746-1747, for Marie Antoinette, doors and decoration above the door, 1787, and for Josephine, wallcovering and furniture.

The wallcovering, a brocaded silk, was rewoven (1968-1986) according to the original pattern which was made in Lyon around 1790 and used for this room in 1805. Its design consisted of four different motifs surrounded by lozenges of water leaves: two motifs of musical instruments, partridges and ruins.

One of two commodes made in 1786, by the cabinetmaker Beneman for the Queen's Gameroom. Spared during the Revolution, the commodes were placed in the Empress's Bedchamber in 1806.

The furniture installed between 1805 and 1807 evokes the Ancien Régime. The bed was made for Marie Antoinette (but she never used it).

During the Empire, the code of etiquette imposed by Napoleon on his second wife, Empress Marie-Louise, required that she be surrounded day and night by her ladies in waiting : « During all of the travels of the court, one of the first ladies always slept in a bedroom next to that of the Empress, and entry to the Empress's bedroom could be obtained only by passing through such lady's bedroom. » (*Memoirs* of the wife of General Durand).

Queen's Boudoir

This room was a private office or boudoir, set up at the demand of Queen Marie Antoinette, at the same time as the Gameroom. The queen spent time here away from the life of the court in the other rooms of the Sovereigns' State Apartments. Only her intimates were admitted to this room.

Wood panel painted after the drawings of the architect Rousseau. The decoration on a silver background is comprised of ancient Pompeian motifs and motifs copied from Raphael's Stanza in the Vatican, as well as floral garlands and simply painted bouquets.

The decoration of the boudoir, completed in less than a year, was ready in time for the last visit of the queen in 1786. It was undoubtedly the architect Rousseau who had the idea to match the furniture to the wainscoting : rolltop writing desk, work table in steel, gilded bronze and mother of pearl (by Riesener), armchairs and stools in gilded and silver-coated wood (by Georges Jacob ; the armchairs are copies).

Throne Room

This was the king's bedroom under the Ancien Régime, the most important room of the palace. Napoleon I transformed the room into the Throne Room in 1808. The ceremonies of presentation and oath-taking normally were held here on Sundays. During a visit in 1810, Madame de Montesquiou was here appointed Governess of the future King of Rome.

The decor is from several different periods. The central part of the ceiling, the lower wainscoting and the doors with pediments date from the middle of the 17th century, while the rest of the wainscoting, sculpted by Verberckt, dates from 1752-1754. The portrait of Louis XIII by the School of Philippe de Champaigne was installed in 1837, recalling the portrait which existed during the Ancien Régime (Napoleon installed his own portrait by Robert Lefèvre).

The present furnishings were installed under Napoleon I. The throne, composed of a crown, two ensigns, a dais and an armchair, were made by Jacob-Dasmalter, based on drawings by Percier and Fontaine.

" Incineration " Passage

This room was installed under the reign of Louis XV, for the king's first valet. According to legend, papers were burned here after the meetings of the Council. Under Louis XVI, the room was used as a wardrobe (for the chamber pot commode).

The wall decorations of flowers, birds, landscapes and arabesques were painted by Alexis Peyrotte in 1753.

The paintings of the virtues and allegories of the seasons and the elements, on the wainscoting and doors, are by Carle Van Loo (in blue) and Jean-Baptiste Pierre (in pink). At left, *Summer*. On opposite page, *Earth*.

The furniture was commissioned by Napoleon I in 1806-1808 (damask, brocade and carpeting were rewoven to match the original).

Council Chamber

Under Louis XV, this room became the chamber of the Council and acquired its present dimensions and form. In this room, the king addressed affairs of the kingdom. Dufort de Cheverny, responsible for the introduction of ambassadors, wrote, around 1755, that at Fontainebleau the king « went hunting everyday except Sundays and holidays. He gave a goodly number of suppers in the small apartments ; the Councils and the work of the ministers occupied the rest of his time ».

From 1751 to 1754, Gabriel oversaw the decoration of this room, which was entrusted to several painters. On the ceiling Boucher painted five canvases: *The Sun Begins its Course and Chases the Night*, and *The Four Seasons*. The semicircular section dates from 1773, and has retained two gilded wood consoles made for this location.

Napoleon I's Imperial Apartment

Emperor's Bedchamber

This room and the adjacent rooms were constructed in a wing built for Louis XVI and constitute what was called the king's interior studies (to distinguish them from the reception rooms). Later, in the time of Napoleon I, they became Napoleon I's Imperial Apartment.

Napoleon made the room into a bedroom in 1808, and it remained the bedroom of all the sovereigns until 1870. The general layout of the wainscoting, fireplace, sculpted door frames and the decorations above the doors (painted by Sauvage) date from 1786. In 1811, the wall decoration was embellished by Moench with paintwork highlighted by gold : imperial bees, victories, etc.

Bed (here, one of
the pediments of the bed
decorated with two
allegorical figures : Justice
and Prosperity), screen
and seating in gilded wood,
trimmed with a chiné velvet
having a motif of flowers
and laurel leaves, rewoven
to match the original
(the background lightened
by embroidery,
as Napoleon wanted it).

The Emperor installed
these furnishings :
ceremonial bed (by Rode),
seating and screen
(by Brion), night table
(Jacob-Desmalter),
and rug (Sallandrouze
of Aubusson).

Emperor's Small Bedroom

The room was, in fact, Napoleon's private study. The iron bed, surmounted by a bedcurtain mount of gilt bronze, was installed in 1811, on the instructions of the Emperor, who wanted to be able to use the room as a second bedroom.

Mechanical desk by Jacob-Desmalter, installed in 1810, greatly valued by Napoleon : by simply pushing the desktop, desk would close, hiding the papers on it without disturbing them.

« The Emperor's life took place in his study ; only there was he at home and his own self ; all the other circumstances of his life could be said to be merely digressions [...] ; there he was an ordinary person, he came to his study in his dressing gown ». (*Memoirs* of Baron Fain, Napoleon's secretary).

Emperor's Private Room

Known as the Abdication Room, this room was where Napoleon on April 6, 1814, decided to abdicate. Baron Fain reported on this occasion the Emperor's remarks to his marshals : « You want some rest, well then, have some ! Alas ! You do not know how much danger and sorrow await you in your featherbeds ! »

Watercolor by Th. Allom (circa 1840) representing the moment when Napoleon prepares to sign his act of abdication on the pedestal table in the center of the room. This scene depicting the Emperor's isolation inspired the legend surrounding the abdication.

Detail of the clock in Sèvres porcelain (Lepaute, 1809). The column is decorated by the twelve hours and the socle by birds symbolizing the different times of day (the owl shown here symbolizes night).

All of the furnishings are those known to the Emperor and were installed in 1808-1809 : gilt wood seats (by Marcion) covered by the same crimson brocade as the wall covering (rewoven to match the original), commodes in black wood (by Jacob-Desmalter), rock crystal chandeliers (by Chaumont), candlesticks and candelabra in gilt bronze (by Thomire) clock in Sèvres porcelain and rug (provided by Bellanger).

Passage to the Emperor's Bathroom

This passage owes its name to the bathroom installed for Napoleon in 1806, in place of the « English privy » of Louis XVI. The mahogany table with drop leaves, by Jacob-Desmalter in 1810, was used by the Emperor for his breakfast.

Mahogany armchair (by Marcion), covered in orange *gourgouran* rewoven in Lyon (this type of silk fabric was frequently used in imperial palaces).

The wall decorations in the bathroom were recreated in 1985-1988. The mahogany chairs (Boulard, 1806) are protected, as during the Empire, by white damask covers (cotton fabric).

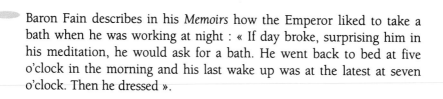 Baron Fain describes in his *Memoirs* how the Emperor liked to take a bath when he was working at night : « If day broke, surprising him in his meditation, he would ask for a bath. He went back to bed at five o'clock in the morning and his last wake up was at the latest at seven o'clock. Then he dressed ».

Room of the Emperor's Aides-de-Camp

The aides-de-camp provided Napoleon with tight security. Twelve in number, one was always nearby the Emperor, and relieved every 24 hours. According to regulations, the furnishings were very simple. The seating (Boulard, 1805) is in wood, painted white, covered in Beauvais tapestry (the present seating installed under the reign of Louis-Philippe replaced the original, which was quite similar). The corner cupboards by Levasseur are from the time of Louis XVI and came from the Bellevue Chateau. The carpet was rewoven to match the original in 1995.

Emperor's Antechamber

The room has retained its Empire furniture, but the wall decoration was changed. The two large paintings replaced the tapestries in 1859 : Vien, *Hector Persuading Paris to Take Arms*, 1783, and Brenet, *Roman Ladies Offering their Jewels to the Senate*, 1785 (at left).

Trinity Chapel

The present structure, built in the 16th century, replaces a chapel of a convent, founded by Saint Louis, which was entrusted to the order of the Trinitarians (hence, its name), to establish a hospital on the premises.

During services, the king and queen generally sat in the gallery, except during major celebrations, when they sat below. The unornamented balconies on both sides of the altar were intended for musicians and singers.

Most of the decor dates from Henri IV and Louis XIII. The restoration undertaken in the 20th century has allowed for the reinstallation of the oval paintings, painted under Louis XVI, between the windows on the first floor.

Many important events occurred in this chapel : the marriage of Louis XV (1725), the baptism of the future Napoleon III (1810), and the marriage of the eldest son of Louis-Philippe (1837).

The patron saints of the royal family are represented on both sides of the altar : here, Saint Charlemagne appears in the likeness of Henri IV.

The high altar (the date of its consecration, 1633, is inscribed in the pediment) is the work of the sculptor Francesco Bordoni who also was responsible for the marble paving on the floor. The altar painting (1642) was painted by Jean Dubois, the son of Ambroise, and represents the Holy Trinity at the moment of the deposition of the Cross.

Bordoni gave the statue of saint Louis the likeness of Louis XIII. The king, who while merely a child closely monitored the decoration of the chapel, holds in his hand the scepter and the hand of Justice.

The decoration of the vault was entrusted by Henri IV to the painter Martin Fréminet. His theme is dedicated to the history of the redemption of man, from the *Appearance of God to Noah* (above the gallery), to *The Annunciation* (above the choir). In the center is the *Christ of the Judgment*. All around are the kings of Judah, the prophets and the virtues.

Small Apartments

Beginning in 1808, Napoleon had these rooms installed in what was then the king's Small Apartments on the ground floor. Napoleon wanted to have two private apartments next to each other, one for himself and the other for Josephine, which later was to be occupied by Marie-Louise.

Méneval's Room

Very simply furnished, this room was used by Napoleon's personal secretary Baron de Méneval, who was succeeded by Baron Fain. The secretary made himself available to the Emperor at all times, by means of a bell connected directly to his room. The secretary was responsible for drafting Napoleon's correspondence.

Emperor's Bedroom

Bed and seating, in the « Egyptian » style, was first placed in Napoleon's bedroom on the first floor. The bed was used by Pope Pius VII at the Tuileries palace in 1804-1805. The furniture was reupholstered in 1858, in Empire chiné velvet, and has so remained.

The geographic clock by the clock-maker Janvier (1751-1835) marks at each instant the true time (in solar time) in every part of France. It was made for Louis XVI in 1791, but it was Napoleon who purchased it in 1806.

Map Room

The Emperor referred to the annex located near his offices as map room, where he could spread his maps and plans, on three joined tables.

Empress's Study Room

The room has retained most of the small pieces of furniture, installed for Empress Marie-Louise in 1810 : writing desk, drawing table, easel, and embroidery frame.

Empress's Second Salon

The decoration of this room was completed for Empress Josephine's last stay in 1809. It is sometimes known as the Yellow Salon because of the grosgrain wall covering having a yellow background and embroidered with amaranthine silk (also covering the seating by Jacob-Desmalter). The console facing the windows is equipped with two bronze rear pilasters to resist the heat emanating from the vent in the stove dating from the first Empire.

Deer Gallery

All of the bronze statues displayed in this gallery formerly decorated the gardens or the façades of the palace. The Laocoon group (at left) was one of the pieces cast at Fontainebleau under François I, based on the antique model.

The gallery, 74 meters long and 7 meters wide, was decorated around 1600, by Louis Poisson with bird's eye views of the forests and royal residences belonging to the crown at the time of Henri IV. By order of Queen Christina of Sweden, the Marquis de Monaldeschi, her chief equerry, was assassinated in this gallery on November 10, 1657, after being convicted of treason.

Empress Eugénie's Salons and the Chinese Museum

In 1863, Empress Eugénie had four rooms installed on the ground floor of the Great Pavilion, in a
location with a charming view of Carp Pond and
the English Garden.

An antechamber, a salon-gallery, and a large salon
called the pond salon, must be crossed to reach the
Chinese Museum. In these rooms, the Empress, in
accordance with the tastes of the period, displayed
objets d'art of the Far East. These objects were
brought back from China during the Franco-British
expedition of 1860 and the sack of the Summer
Palace, or received as gifts from ambassadors from
Siam during their reception at Fontainebleau in 1861.
The comfortable seating, the piano, the billiard tables
in the salons, and the specially conceived display
cabinets in the Chinese Museum give a distinctive
atmosphere to these rooms intended for relaxation
and intimate court receptions.

From the Summer Palace,
these golden vases
(China, 18th century) were
acquired by Napoleon III
and given to the Empress
on her saint's day.

Great plate in enameled
porcelain, in the green
family, Kangxi period
1662-1722.

Ewers in gold cloisonné
enamel, Qianlong period,
1736-1795.

Octave Feuillet, while he was palace librarian, described the receptions
which he attended in these salons during the residence of the court in
1868 : « Having returned to the palace, we tried the « round dance of the
Nantes Bridge » in the Chinese Salon [...]. Mademoiselle Louise d'Albe
came to sit next to me with her solitaire game [...]. I broke Madame Redel's
fan, when the Empress called us to the adjacent salon for tea ».

Coral Lion, Qianlong period, 1736-1795.

Replica of the crown of the kings of Siam, gift to Napoleon III, adorned with rubies, emeralds and pearls (below left). Stupa in gilt copper, Qianlong period circa 1770 (below).

Paintbrush rest in white jade, China 17th-18th century.

Buddhas of the past, present and future, tapestries, Qianlong period, 1736-1795.

Chimera in cloisonné enamel, Qianlong period 1736-1796 (above).

Dish in blue and white porcelain, China, 15th century (left).

For the wall decorations of the Chinese Museum, the panels of the lacquered screens, from the furniture storage (China 18th century), were used and the cloisonné enamels were set into chandeliers or girandoles.

« After which we entered the Chinese salon for tea. The curios are magnificent : gold and enamel pagodas, enormous idols, gigantic vases, sparkling in the glow of the chandeliers and the girandoles » (Octave Feuillet).

Napoleon I Museum

Installed in the Louis XV wing, the Napoleon I Museum (inaugurated in 1986) is comprised of collections relating to Napoleon and his family at the time of the Empire (1804-1815). Paintings, sculptures, furnishings, objets d'art, articles of clothing, arms and ornaments are presented in an appropriate setting or in display cases.

The diversity of the works allows for the evocation, in turn, of Napoleon the Emperor of the French and King of Italy, the splendor of the imperial table, the gifts made to the Emperor, his life on military campaign, and his daily life. The Empress Marie-Louise, the King of Rome, and Napoleon's mother, brothers and sisters all appear through their portraits or the objects that belonged to them.

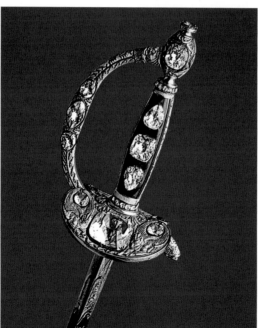

Napoleon in his Coronation Costume (by Gérard). Only the tunic, the white silk sash embroidered with gold and the sword remain today.

Snuffbox containing a gold leaf of the Crown of the coronation, given by Napoleon to the painter Isabey.

Sword of the First Consul, later the Emperor, called the Coronation Sword, originally adorned with diamonds, including the famous Regent Diamond (today in the Louvre).

Plate of Sèvres porcelain (1808-1809) in the personal table service of the Emperor, representing one of Napoleon's arabian horses.

Marriage banquet of Napoleon and Marie-Louise (April 2, 1810) in the performance room in the Tuileries palace (by Casanova, son).
The table decorations include some of the grand vermeil, a gift from the city of Paris in 1804.
In the front of the table, are placed the Emperor's and Empress's serving ships.

Napoleon personally had very simple tastes. Luxury was reserved for ceremonies and the splendor of the throne. The Emperor on military campaigns generally wore over his uniform a woolen cloth overcoat, either grey (below) or green, strong enough to last three years.

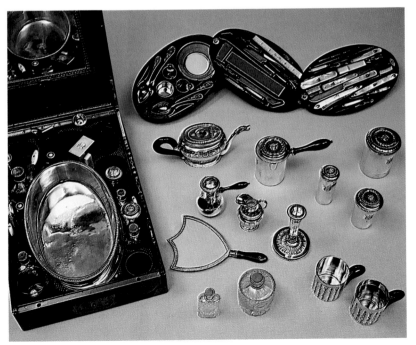

The Emperor's serving ship in vermeil, by the silversmith Auguste (Paris, 1804). Traditional symbol of the sovereign's table, it was used to hold spices or napkins.

Emperor's travel case, delivered in 1809, by the silversmith Biennais. Napoleon had many such cases, which held his toiletries, table service or work and writing materials.

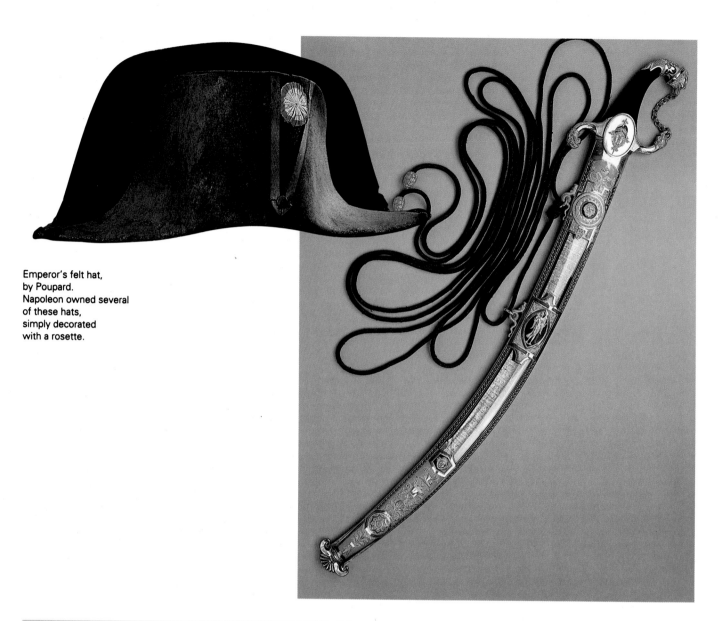

Emperor's felt hat,
by Poupard.
Napoleon owned several
of these hats,
simply decorated
with a rosette.

Sabre of Napoleon called the
Emperor's Sabre (because of
the names of the emperors of
Rome and the Holy Empire
engraved on the blade). The
setting, and the sheath in gold
and rock crystal, were made
by Boutet and Biennais (1798).

Tea service in Sèvres
porcelain (1812),
which belonged to
Empress Marie-Louise,
decorated with scenes
representing Cupid's
pains and pleasures.

Empress Marie-Louise's
gold pendant watch
delivered by jeweller
Nitot 1813.

King of Rome's cradle,
in elm and gilt bronze,
by Thomire and Duterme
(1811). It appeared in
the bedchamber
of the King of Rome
in the Tuileries palace.

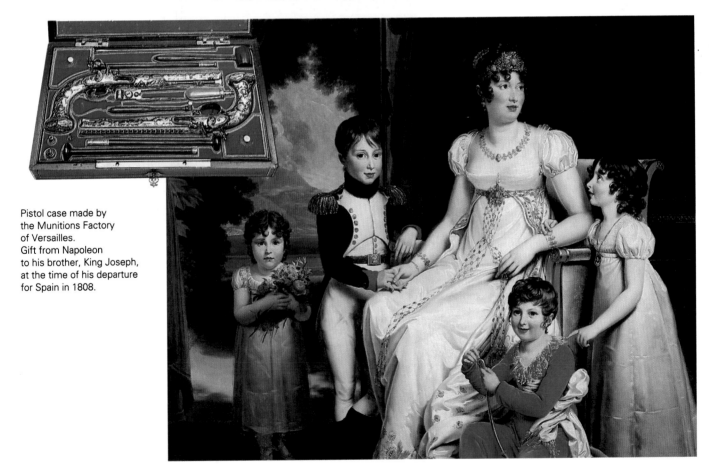

Pistol case made by
the Munitions Factory
of Versailles.
Gift from Napoleon
to his brother, King Joseph,
at the time of his departure
for Spain in 1808.

Napoleon placed most of his brothers and sisters on the different thrones of Europe that he conquered or created. He enthroned : Joseph, first in Naples, later in Spain, Louis in Holland, Jérôme in Westphalia, Elisa in Tuscany, and Caroline in Naples (above, her portrait with her four children, with Mt. Vesuvius and the Bay of Naples in the background, by Gérard).

Gardens

François I was responsible for creating the gardens, where water has always played an important role. The gardens were substantially transformed by Henri IV, Louis XIV and Napoleon.

English Garden

It assumed its present form around 1812, laid out in the tradition of English gardens of the 18th century. Previously, several gardens were successively planted on the site, among them the Pine Grove planted by François I. Today, the garden is graced by plane trees, sequoias, tulip trees, and cypress trees of which the oldest were planted during the Second Empire.

The stream was created by the architect Hurtault and winds across the garden towards the far end where a basin marks the site of the legendary Beautiful Water (*Belle Eau*) fountain.

Two bronzes installed in 1813, in front of the Louis XV wing, stand out from among the sculptures which embellish the garden : the *Fighting Gladiator* and the *Dying Gladiator* (cast in the 17th century based on the antique models). At the end of the wing is found the famous Grotto of the Pines created for François I around 1543.

Carp Pond

The pond owes its name to the famous carp whose presence at Fontainebleau goes back to Henri IV. The king received sixty of them as a gift from Duke Charles of Lorraine. The ceremony in which the king touched those afflicted with scrofula, took place in the avenue which runs alongside the west side of the pond.

From the 16th century, the pond served as a setting for celebrations, water tournaments and fireworks. The pavilion in the middle was constructed under Louis XIV in 1622, by Le Vau (and restored under Napoleon). Suppers were held there for the king and the royal family. In 1717, the Czar Peter the Great and his retinue could be seen there and according to Saint-Simon, « they had amply drunk and eaten ».

Grand Parterre

Located to the east of the pond and below the path (called the de Maintenon path) which leads to the Golden Entrance, this French garden retains the layout which Le Vau and Le Notre gave it in 1660-1664. It replaced the large garden of François I, of which a part served as a playing field, and the one which Henri IV had planted by the landscape architect Claude Mollet and the fountain engineer Tommaso Francini.

The Golden Entrance, built in 1528, served as the entrance for Charles the Fifth on his arrival in 1539.

74

From the Grand Parterre, the view encompasses the part of the palace extending from the Golden Entrance, with its upper level Italian style loggias, to the Kitchen Courtyard, and includes the Ballroom with large bay windows, the Saint Saturnin Chapel and the Dauphin's Entrance (covered by a dome). In the foreground, the round basin is decorated with a statue of the Tiber.

Canal

From the top of the basin of waterfalls built under Louis XIV (in ruins from the 18th century, it was entirely rebuilt in the 19th century), the view extends over the canal, which is nearly 1200 meters long. In the middle of the basin, *Eagle Defending its Prey* by Cain, was installed in 1866.

The filling of the canal with water in the month of May 1609, was the object of a wager between Henri IV and one of his courtiers, the Marshal of Bassompierre : « The king wagered one thousand écus against me that in two days it would be full, and in eight days, it still was not full ».

Park

Below the Grand Parterre stretches a park of more than 80 hectares, enclosed by walls and pierced by rectilinear paths. Established under Henri IV, the park is crossed by the grand canal, which the king had excavated from 1606 to 1609.

The Napoleon Fountain in the north of the park was erected in the Second Empire and is the source of a stream which flows out in cascades. Very popular, the fountain has long served the residents of Fontainebleau.

The king's vine arbor which covers the wall enclosing the north park was originally planted under Louis XV. It produces a famous grape, Fontainebleau chasselas.

Under Louis XIV, the promenades along the park pathways and around the canal were a traditional distraction of the court. *The Mercure de France* observed : « There was a promenade (October 1, 1707) of approximately 150 ladies dressed as amazons and whose clothing was magnificent, and 94 coaches were counted. ».

Diana's Garden

This garden is located next to the town and owes its name to the statue of Diana which decorates the fountain erected under Henri IV. The present statue dates from 1684 and replaced in 1813 the original bronze by Barthélemy Prieur (currently on display in the Deer Gallery).

The fountain engineer Francini was responsible for the arrangement of the dogs and deer heads spitting water (by Pierre Biard 1603).

The garden today
is arranged as an English
garden, in keeping with
its style under Napoleon
and Louis-Philippe.

The gate with Egyptian
caryatids, built under
François I, provided
access to the arms
cabinet of Henri II.

In the 16th century, certain bronzes based on the antique model and cast under the direction of Primaticcio, were placed in this garden. The *Laocoon* and the *Sleeping Ariane* are currently displayed in the Deer Gallery. The renown of these statues earned Fontainebleau the name of « New Rome ».

Photo Credits:

RMN/Lagiewski : p. 15 t, 16-17, 18 t, 24-25, 27 b,
28 l, 28-29 b, 29 t, 32, 33, 34, 35, 37, 38 t and r, 39, 40,
41, 43, 44, 45, 46, 47, 50, 51, 52, 53, 54, 55, 56-57, 58,
59, 60, 61, 62, 66, 67, 72, 73, 74, 75, 77 t, 78-79.
RMN/Blot : 14-15, 22-23, 28-29t, 29b, 63, 66, 73t.
RMN/Schormans-Arnaudet : 15 b.
RMN/Arnaudet : 20.
RMN/Bernard : 36-37, 78.
RMN/Willy : 25r, 26b, 27t, 30, 31, 36.
RMN/Derenne : 38t, 42, 59b.
RMN/Beck-Coppola : 57b.
Art Lys/Ryo : 15b, 17r and b, 18 b, 19, 77 b.
Art Lys/Crapet : 8-9.
Art Lys/Février : couverture.

Editorial coordinator : Denis Kilian
Editorial follow-up : Christian Ryo
Layout : Vincent Grousson
Printing : Pierre Kegels, Christian Ryo
Maps : Thierry Lebreton, Dominique Bissière

Achevé d'imprimer le 15 Août 1999,
par Hérissey à Évreux.

Dépôt légal Août 1999.

ISBN 2-85495-087-9

45 F